Other humor books available from InterVarsity Press:

All God's Children Got Gum in Their Hair by Steve Phelps
Amusing Grace by Ed Koehler
As the Church Turns by Ed Koehler
Church Is Stranger Than Fiction by Mary Chambers
Climbing the Church Walls by Rob Portlock
It Came from Beneath the Pew by Rob Suggs
Less Than Entirely Sanctified by Doug Hall
Murphy Goes to Church by Steve Dennie and Rob Suggs
Murphy's Laws of Parenting by Steve Dennie and Rob Suggs
Off the Church Wall by Rob Portlock
101 Things to Do with a Dull Church by Martin Wroe and Adrian Reith
The Potluck Hall of Fame by David Dickerson and Mary Chambers
Preacher from the Black Lagoon by Rob Suggs
Reborn to Be Wild by Doug Hall
Way Off the Church Wall by Rob Portlock

Families Off the Wall

Rob Portlock

INTERVARSITY PRESS
DOWNERS GROVE, ILLINOIS 60515

InterVarsity Press® is the book-publishing division of InterVarsity Christian Fellowship®, a student movement active on campus at hundreds of universities, colleges and schools of nursing in the United States of America, and a member movement of the International Fellowship of Evangelical Students. For information about local and regional activities, write Public Relations Dept., InterVarsity Christian Fellowship, 6400 Schroeder Rd., P.O. Box 7895, Madison, WI 53707-7895.

Cover illustration: Rob Portlock

ISBN 0-8308-1823-5

Printed in the United States of America ∞

Library of Congress Cataloging-in-Publication Data has been requested.

17	16	15	14	13	12	11	10	9	8	7	6	5	4	3	2	1
08	07	06	05	04	03	02	01	00	99	98	97	96	95	94		

"I think it says Jimmy doesn't like kindergarten."

PORTLOCK

Peggy was virtually assured the PTA seat opening when during her interview she nailed
a triple salchow followed by a double lutz.

"Has anyone seen the cat?"

"That was ten times better than a roller coaster!"

"I still say she's too overprotective."

PORTLOCK

"See . . . I told you not to touch that button!"

"Looks like a phone message from one of my teenagers."

"Daddy, I think Mommy wants you."

PORTLOCK

"Paper, plastic or blue suede?"

"Wow. Look. It's one of Mom and Dad's antiques!"

"Mirror, mirror on the wall, who's the . . ."

"Personally, I also prefer briefs to boxers."

"We'd like to go to a Caribbean island where there are no diapers."

"O.K., O.K. I'm guilty. It was more than ten items."

"No, he didn't hurt himself using the new exercise machine. He hurt himself bringing it in from the car."

NEW CARS

PORTLOCK

"We've decided not to buy the minivan, but we'll take two dozen of these cookies."

"Get a video of me taking the banana from this big gorilla."

PORTLOCK

"The remote control doesn't work here, Dad."

"Sorry to bother Your Highness. The queen says you need to come and change the little prince's diapers."

"Line 1, Bachman and Jones on hold. Line 2, your stockbroker on standby. Line 3, your ex-boyfriend on ignore."

"Daddy has admission shock."

PORTLOCK

FREE
BUNGIE
JUMPING
AFTER SERVICE

PORTLOCK

"We'd like to go to the Holy Land with a quick stopover at the French Riviera."

"I enjoyed the 8 a.m. service. How about you?"

"No, I'm sorry, Mrs. Perkins. We don't have women's day here."

"That's the last time we let Ralph watch a horror movie with us."

"Betty says she's finally found a diet that works."

"It's good to finally meet you, Mr. Farnsworth."

"I think it's time to check out the projected cost of Bible college eighteen years from now."

FIRST WEEK OF HOME SCHOOL DIDN'T GO WELL

"No, children. You won't be singing 'Layla' today in Sunday school!"

"Do you think our relationship is too businesslike?"

"Have you noticed? Mom's been a little standoffish lately."

"Hey, don't take all the cold water!"

"Honey, wake up; you're using the remote in your sleep again."

PORTLOCK

"I hate playing miniature golf with the Ketelsens."

PHOTOS
$ 2.50 ea.
FOOT PRINTS
$15.00 ea.

ZOO

PORTLOCK

The family, dog, house, picket fence and satellite dish

PORTLOCK

"Mr. Disney?"

PARENT'S DREAM

"Sorry, Mom. We thought this was the kitchen."

"I'm sorry, doctor. I forgot to tell him how much Susie's braces would be."

"O.K. You fax me the lyrics to 'Mary Had a Little Lamb,' and I'll fax you 'Three Blind Mice.'"

"I knew we shouldn't have let the kids have the house for the weekend!"

"Flies again?"

"Brutus, that's a no-no!"

"He followed me. Can I keep him?"

PORTLOCK

"O.K. That's it. No more sugar for you!"

"O.K., maybe we won't change to decaf just yet."

"No, Billy. David and Goliath is not out in Nintendo yet."

"Ha, ha, ha! I'm not falling for that again."

"Time for 'quiet time,' children."

"Looks like Dad can't find the remote again."

"As your realtor I have to inform you that Tommy Brown at 264 is learning the drums."

"Hi, Mom, what's for dinner?"

"I'm worried about what the doctor told me today. He said to stop worrying about everything."

IT HIT DEBBIE AT THAT MOMENT. SHE WAS ABOUT TO MARRY A <u>REAL</u> CLOW'N.

"For crying out loud, Bess, *relax!*"

MARRIAGE FORECAST

PORTLOCK

"How much to just touch and smell?"

"No, young man. You may not say your bedtime prayers by inputting them into your computer!"

". . . And do you, William, take Deborah to be your wife?"

"They're playing our song!"

"I'm so glad you decided not to play golf today."

"Ms. Barret, is anyone missing a baby?"

JUST CAME TO PLEASE SPOUSE ROOM

PORTLOCK

It was said that the Nelsons did everything together.

THE SMITHS' MARRIAGE GOT OFF TO A BAD START

PORTLOCK

"Here's the last church I pastored at."

PORTLOCK

"I thought I told you kids to stay out of the super glue."

Baby Discovering Lungs

"See, I told you we'd make it to church on time this week."

"My mom just hates losing at Nintendo."

"He always gets whatever he wants for Christmas."

"Now I'd like to do another little song I wrote. It's called 'Potty Training Blues.'"

PORTLOCK

"And then Little Red Riding Hood said to the Big Bad Wolf, 'That's sexual harassment. See you in court!'"

"That's the last time I let Bobby get tires on the station wagon."

PORTLOCK

"Hey, don't get too comfy!"

"Can we have a minute to discuss the sticker price?"

"Mr. George, would you ask your children to wait in the lobby?"

"I don't know where the kids are. I thought you were watching them."

"I can't wait to grow up so I can say 'hallelujah' in church."

VENUS

NEPTUNE

MARS

SATURN

MERCURY

EARTH

JUPITER

PLUTO

URANUS

LOST SOCK

"I love the special effects on these Christian cable stations!"

PORTLOCK

"Have you noticed? Things aren't the same since Mom and Dad switched to decaf."

"Does Mom seem a little tense?"

PORTLOCK

"I hate the way he says 'I'm hungry.'"

"I hate it when Mom does that."